THE CLASSIC
RIDER WAITE SMITH
TAROT

THE CLASSIC
RIDER WAITE SMITH
TAROT

Arthur Edward Waite

ABRIDGED EDITION

Colour-enhanced cards from 1909 Rider Waite
deck copyright Arcturus Publishing.
All other images courtesy of Shutterstock.

This edition published in 2025 by Arcturus Publishing Limited
26/27 Bickels Yard, 151–153 Bermondsey Street,
London SE1 3HA

Copyright © Arcturus Holdings Limited

All rights reserved. No part of this publication may be reproduced, stored in a retrieval system, or transmitted, in any form or by any means, electronic, mechanical, photocopying, recording or otherwise, without prior written permission in accordance with the provisions of the Copyright Act 1956 (as amended). Any person or persons who do any unauthorised act in relation to this publication may be liable to criminal prosecution and civil claims for damages.

AD010373UK

Printed in China

Contents

INTRODUCTION 6

1. THE TRUMPS MAJOR AND THEIR INNER SYMBOLISM 9

2. THE LESSER ARCANA
   THE SUIT OF WANDS 20
   THE SUIT OF CUPS 24
   THE SUIT OF SWORDS 28
   THE SUIT OF PENTACLES 31

3. THE GREATER ARCANA AND THEIR DIVINATORY MEANINGS 34

4. SOME ADDITIONAL MEANINGS OF THE LESSER ARCANA 37

5. THE RECURRENCE OF CARDS IN DEALING 42

6. THE ART OF TAROT DIVINATION 44

7. AN ANCIENT CELTIC METHOD OF DIVINATION 45

INTRODUCTION

First published in 1909, the Rider Waite Smith (RWS) is one of the most popular Tarot decks in the world, and the inspiration for the majority of decks on the market today. The deck was created by the artist Pamela Colman Smith (also known as Pixie) under the direction of the famous mystic, Arthur Edward Waite. Published by William Rider, it was known for many years simply as the 'Rider Waite' deck—overlooking the importance of Smith's artistic input. Today, the modern Tarot community includes her name in the title to acknowledge the significant contribution of her artwork to the deck's popularity and longevity.

Born in London, to a Jamaican mother and American father, Smith was an unconventional, bohemian artist, known for going into a trance and channelling drawings while listening to music. She, along with Waite, was a member of the secret society, the Hermetic Order of the Golden Dawn. Waite was a prolific author and scholar of the occult, who also translated and reissued several mystical and alchemical works.

Before the *Rider Waite Smith*, most Tarot decks illustrated the Major Arcana and Court Cards, but used simple groups of cups, coins, wands and swords on the Minor Arcana. Waite wanted to create a fully illustrated deck and suggested that Smith examined the fifteenth century *Sola Busca* deck for inspiration. Showing characters and scenes on the Minor Arcana revolutionised the Tarot, making it relatable and accessible. This was further helped by *The Pictorial Key to the Tarot*, the guide that was written by Waite to explain the ideas behind the esoteric symbolism in Smith's artwork, and published in 1910.

The Key constantly encourages the reader to search the cards for meaning. The interpretations often start with a description of the picture, ensuring that you examine every detail. *"On one side a ship is riding and on the other a dolphin is leaping,"* Waite writes, under the King of Cups.

Had you noticed the dolphin? You look at the card again and see it leaping from the choppy waters. It reminds you of the fish peeking out on the Page of Cups ... Was the water in that picture stormy or calm? You find that card to compare them and soon find that you are looking at others, searching for clues that will deepen your understanding. You uncover repeated symbols—columns, clouds, roses, lilies, stars, fruit, mountains—and note their similarities and differences across the deck. Are the flowers growing on the ground or embroidered on cloth? How close is the castle? How many rays does the sun have?

This is the beauty of Smith's densely-packed designs—even the smallest dot or line has meaning, from the skull hidden in the lines of the chalice on the Seven of Cups to the tiny horned snail on the Nine of Pentacles. Waite and Smith created a deck that was accessible to beginners but remained fascinating for experienced readers. There are always new things to notice, even after using the cards for many years.

This guide is a heavily abridged edition of *The Key*, cutting through much of the denunciation of other authors (on occasion, Waite even berated his own writings under a nom de plume!) and concentrating on the rich explanations of the symbolism of the cards. Ultimately, it is the artwork of the cards themselves that continues to connect with tarot enthusiasts.

Xanna Eve Chown

I. THE TRUMPS MAJOR AND THEIR INNER SYMBOLISM

I The Magician

A youthful figure in the robe of a magician, having the countenance of divine Apollo, with a smile of confidence. Above his head is the mysterious sign of the Holy Spirit, the sign of life, like an endless cord, forming the figure 8 in a horizontal position. About his waist is a serpent-cincture, the serpent appearing to devour its own tail. In the Magician's right hand is a wand raised towards heaven, while the left hand is pointing to the earth. It shews the descent of grace, virtue and light, drawn from things above and derived to things below. The suggestion throughout is therefore the possession and communication of the Powers and Gifts of the Spirit. This card signifies the divine motive in humans, reflecting God, the will in the liberation of its union with that which is above.

II The High Priestess

She has the lunar crescent at her feet, a horned diadem on her head, with a globe in the middle place. The scroll in her hands is inscribed with the word Tora. It is partly covered by her mantle, to shew that some things are implied and some spoken. She is seated between the white and black pillars of the mystic Temple, and the veil is behind her: it is embroidered with palms and pomegranates. The vestments are flowing and gauzy, and the mantle suggests light. She has been called Occult Science on the threshold of the Sanctuary of Isis, but she is really the Secret Church. There are some respects in which this card is the highest and holiest of the Greater Arcana.

III The Empress

A stately figure, seated, having rich vestments and royal aspect, as of a daughter of heaven and earth. Her diadem is of twelve stars, gathered in a cluster. The symbol of Venus is on the shield which rests near her. A field of corn is ripening in front of her, and beyond there is a fall of water. The sceptre which she bears is surmounted by the globe of this world. She is the inferior Garden of Eden, the Earthly Paradise, all that is symbolized by the visible house of man. There are also certain aspects in which she has been correctly described as desire and the wings thereof, as the woman clothed with the sun, as Gloria Mundi and the veil of the Sanctum Sanctorum; but she is not, I may add, the soul that has attained wings. She is above all things universal fecundity. In another order of ideas, the card of the Empress signifies the door by which an entrance is obtained into this life, as into the Garden of Venus, and then the way which leads out therefrom, into that which is beyond.

IV The Emperor

He has a form of the *Crux ansata* for his sceptre and a globe in his left hand. He is a crowned monarch—commanding, stately, seated on a throne, the arms of which are fronted by rams' heads. He is executive and realization, the power of this world, here clothed with the highest of its natural attributes. He is the virile power, to which the Empress responds, and in this sense it is he who seeks to remove the Veil of Isis. It should be understood that this card and that of the Empress do not precisely represent the condition of married life, though this state is implied. On the surface, as I have indicated, they stand for mundane royalty, uplifted on the seats of the mighty; but above this there is the suggestion of another presence. They signify also—and the male figure especially—the higher kingship, occupying the intellectual throne. Hereof is the lordship of thought rather than of the animal world.

V THE HIEROPHANT

He wears the triple crown and is seated between two pillars, but they are not those of the Temple which is guarded by the High Priestess. In his left hand he holds a sceptre terminating in the triple cross, and with his right hand he gives the well-known ecclesiastical sign which is called that of esotericism. It is noticeable in this connexion that the High Priestess makes no sign. At his feet are the crossed keys, and two priestly ministers kneel before him. He has been usually called the Pope, which is a particular application of the more general office that he symbolizes. He is the ruling power of external religion, as the High Priestess is the prevailing genius of the esoteric, withdrawn power. He is the order and the head of the recognized hierarchy, which is the reflection of another and greater hierarchic order; but it may so happen that the pontiff forgets the significance of this his symbolic state and acts as if he contained within his proper measures all that his sign signifies or his symbol seeks to shew forth.

VI THE LOVERS

The sun shines in the zenith, and beneath is a great winged figure with arms extended, pouring down influences. In the foreground are two human figures, unveiled before each other, as if Adam and Eve when they first occupied the paradise of the earthly body. Behind the man is the Tree of Life, bearing twelve fruits, and the Tree of the Knowledge of Good and Evil is behind the woman; the serpent is twining round it. The figures suggest youth, virginity, innocence and love before it is contaminated by gross material desire. This is in all simplicity the card of human love. The suggestion in respect of the woman is that she signifies that attraction towards the sensitive life which carries within it the idea of the Fall of Man, but she is the working of a Secret Law of Providence than a conscious temptress. The card is therefore in its way another intimation concerning the great mystery of womanhood.

VII The Chariot

THE CHARIOT

He is conquest on all planes—in the mind, in science, in progress, in certain trials of initiation. He has thus replied to the sphinx, and it is on this account that I have accepted the variation of Eliphas Levi; two sphinxes thus draw his chariot. He is above all things triumphant in the mind. It is to be understood for this reason (a) that the question of the sphinx is concerned with a Mystery of Nature and not of the world of Grace, to which the charioteer could offer no answer; (b) that the planes of his conquest are manifest or external and not within himself; (c) that the liberation which he effects may leave himself in the bondage of the logical understanding; (d) that the tests of initiation through which he has passed in triumph are to be understood physically or rationally; and (e) that if he came to the pillars of that Temple between which the High Priestess is seated, he could not open the scroll called Tora, nor if she questioned him could he answer.

VIII Strength or Fortitude

STRENGTH

A woman, over whose head there broods the same symbol of life which we have seen in the card of the Magician, is closing the jaws of a lion. The only point in which this design differs from the conventional presentations is that her beneficent fortitude has already subdued the lion, which is being led by a chain of flowers. For reasons which satisfy myself, this card has been interchanged with that of justice, which is usually numbered eight. As the variation carries nothing with it which will signify to the reader, there is no cause for explanation. Fortitude, in one of its most exalted aspects, is connected with the Divine Mystery of Union; the virtue, of course, operates in all planes, and hence draws on all in its symbolism. It connects also with *innocentia inviolata*, and with the strength which resides in contemplation. These higher meanings are, however, matters of inference.

IX The Hermit

The variation from the conventional models in this card is only that the lamp is not enveloped partially in the mantle of its bearer, who blends the idea of the Ancient of Days with the Light of the World. It is a star which shines in the lantern. I have said that this is a card of attainment, and to extend this conception the figure is seen holding up his beacon on an eminence. Therefore the Hermit is not, as Court de Gebelin explained, a wise man in search of truth and justice; nor is he, as a later explanation proposes, an especial example of experience. His beacon intimates that "where I am, you also may be." It is further a card which is understood quite incorrectly when it is connected with the idea of occult isolation. This is one of the frivolous renderings which we owe to Eliphas Levi. It did not refer to the intended concealment of the Instituted Mysteries, much less of their substitutes, but to the truth that the Divine Mysteries secure their own protection from those who are unprepared.

X Wheel of Fortune

In this symbol I have again followed the reconstruction of Eliphas Levi, who has furnished several variants. It is legitimate—as I have intimated—to use Egyptian symbolism when this serves our purpose, provided that no theory of origin is implied therein. I have, however, presented Typhon in his serpent form. The symbolism is, of course, not exclusively Egyptian, as the four Living Creatures of Ezekiel occupy the angles of the card, and the wheel itself follows other indications of Levi in respect of Ezekiel's vision, as illustrative of the particular Tarot Key. With the French occultist, and in the design itself, the symbolic picture stands for the perpetual motion of a fluidic universe and for the flux of human life. The Sphinx is the equilibrium therein. The transliteration of Taro as Rota is inscribed on the wheel, counterchanged with the letters of the Divine Name—to shew that Providence is implied through all.

XI Justice

It will be seen that the figure is seated between pillars, like the High Priestess, and on this account it seems desirable to indicate that the moral principle which deals unto every man according to his works—while, of course, it is in strict analogy with higher things—differs in its essence from the spiritual justice which is involved in the idea of election. The latter belongs to a mysterious order of Providence, in virtue of which it is possible for certain men to conceive the idea of dedication to the highest things. The operation of this is like the breathing of the Spirit, where it wills, and we have no canon of criticism or ground of explanation concerning it. It is analogous to the possession of the fairy gifts and the high gifts and the gracious gifts of the poet: we have them or have not, and their presence is as much a mystery as their absence. The law of Justice is not however involved by either alternative. In conclusion, the pillars of Justice open into one world and the pillars of the High Priestess into another.

XII The Hanged Man

The gallows from which he is suspended forms a Tau cross, while the figure—from the position of the leg—forms a fylfot cross. There is a nimbus about the head of the seeming martyr. It should be noted (1) that the tree of sacrifice is living wood, with leaves thereon; (2) that the face expresses deep entrancement, not suffering; (3) that the figure, as a whole, suggests life in suspension, but life and not death. It is a card of profound significance, but all the significance is veiled. One of his editors suggests that Eliphas Levi did not know the meaning, which is unquestionably nor did the editor himself. It has been called falsely a card of martyrdom, a card of prudence, a card of the Great Work, a card of duty; but we may exhaust all published interpretations and find only vanity. I will say very simply on my own part that it expresses the relation, in one of its aspects, between the Divine and the Universe.

XIII Death

The veil of life is perpetuated in change, transformation and passage from lower to higher, and this is more fitly represented in the rectified Tarot by one of the apocalyptic visions than by the crude notion of the reaping skeleton. Behind it lies the whole world of ascent in the spirit. The mysterious horseman moves slowly, bearing a black banner emblazoned with the Mystic Rose, which signifies life. Between two pillars on the verge of the horizon there shines the sun of immortality. The horseman carries no visible weapon, but king and child and maiden fall before him, while a prelate with clasped hands awaits his end. The natural transit of man to the next stage of his being is one form of his progress, but the exotic and almost unknown entrance, while still in this life, into the state of mystical death is a change in the form of consciousness and the passage into a state to which ordinary death is neither the path nor gate. The existing explanations are, on the whole, better than usual: rebirth, creation, destination, renewal.

XIV Temperance

A winged angel, with the sign of the sun upon his forehead and on his breast the square and triangle of the septenary. I speak of him in the masculine sense, but the figure is neither male nor female. It is held to be pouring the essences of life from chalice to chalice. It has one foot upon the earth and one upon waters, thus illustrating the nature of the essences. A direct path goes up to certain heights on the verge of the horizon, and above there is a great light, through which a crown is seen vaguely. Hereof is some part of the Secret of Eternal Life, as it is possible to man in his incarnation. It is untrue to say that the figure symbolizes the genius of the sun, though it is the analogy of solar light, realized in the third part of our human triplicity. It is called Temperance fantastically, because, when the rule of it obtains in our consciousness, it tempers, combines and harmonises the psychic and material natures.

XV The Devil

The Horned Goat of Mendes, with wings like those of a bat, is standing on an altar. The right hand is upraised and extended, being the reverse of that benediction which is given by the Hierophant in the fifth card. In the left hand there is a great flaming torch, inverted towards the earth. A reversed pentagram is on the forehead. There is a ring in front of the altar, from which two chains are carried to the necks of two figures, male and female. These are analogous with those of the fifth card, as if Adam and Eve after the Fall. Hereof is the chain and fatality of the material life. The figures are tailed, to signify the animal nature, but there is human intelligence in the faces, and he who is exalted above them is not to be their master forever. Even now, he is also a bondsman, sustained by the evil that is in him and blind to the liberty of service. It signifies the Dweller on the Threshold without the Mystical Garden once those are driven forth who have eaten the forbidden fruit.

XVI The Tower

Occult explanations attached to this card are meagre and mostly disconcerting. It is said that it contains the first allusion to a material building, but I do not conceive that the Tower is more or less material than the pillars which we have met with in three previous cases. I see nothing to warrant Papus in supposing that it is literally the fall of Adam, but there is more in favour of his alternative—that it signifies the materialization of the spiritual word. The bibliographer Christian imagines that it is the downfall of the mind, seeking to penetrate the mystery of God. I agree rather with Grand Orient that it is the ruin of the House of We, when evil has prevailed therein, and above all that it is the rending of a House of Doctrine. I understand that the reference is, however, to a House of Falsehood. It illustrates also in the most comprehensive way the old truth that "except the Lord build the house, they labour in vain that build it."

XVII The Star

A great, radiant star of eight rays, surrounded by seven lesser stars—also of eight rays. The female figure in the foreground is entirely naked. Her left knee is on the land and her right foot upon the water. She pours Water of Life from two great ewers, irrigating sea and land. Behind her is rising ground and on the right a shrub or tree, whereon a bird alights. The figure expresses eternal youth and beauty. The star is *l'etoile flamboyante*, which appears in Masonic symbolism, but has been confused therein. That which the figure communicates to the living scene is the substance of the heavens and the elements. It has been said truly that the mottoes of this card are "Waters of Life freely" and "Gifts of the Spirit." On other planes it has been certified as immortality and interior light. For the majority of prepared minds, the figure will appear as the type of Truth unveiled, glorious in undying beauty, pouring on the waters of the soul some measure of her priceless possession.

XVIII The Moon

The card represents life of the imagination apart from life of the spirit. The path between the towers is the issue into the unknown. The dog and wolf are the fears of the natural mind in the presence of that place of exit, when there is only reflected light to guide it. The intellectual light is a reflection and beyond it is the unknown mystery which it cannot shew forth. It illuminates our animal nature, types of which are represented below—the dog, the wolf and that which comes up out of the deeps, the nameless and hideous tendency which is lower than the savage beast. It strives to attain manifestation, symbolized by crawling from the abyss of water to the land, but as a rule it sinks back whence it came. The face of the mind directs a calm gaze upon the unrest below; the dew of thought falls; the message is: Peace, be still; and it may be that there shall come a calm upon the animal nature.

XIX The Sun

The naked child mounted on a white horse and displaying a red standard has been mentioned already as the better symbolism connected with this card. It is the destiny of the Supernatural East and the great and holy light which goes before the endless procession of humanity, coming out from the walled garden of the sensitive life and passing on the journey home. The card signifies, therefore, the transit from the manifest light of this world, represented by the glorious sun of earth, to the light of the world to come, which goes before aspiration and is typified by the heart of a child. But the last allusion is again the key to a different form or aspect of the symbolism. The sun is that of consciousness in the spirit—the direct as the antithesis of the reflected light. The characteristic type of humanity has become a little child therein—a child in the sense of simplicity and innocence in the sense of wisdom. In that simplicity, he bears the seal of Nature and of Art; in that innocence, he signifies the restored world.

XX Judgement

The great angel is here encompassed by clouds, but he blows his bannered trumpet. It should be noted that all the figures are as one in the wonder, adoration and ecstasy expressed by their attitudes. It is the card which registers the accomplishment of the great work of transformation in answer to the summons of the Supernal—which summons is heard and answered from within. What is that within us which does sound a trumpet and all that is lower in our nature rises in response—almost in a moment, almost in the twinkling of an eye? Let the card continue to depict, for those who can see no further, the Last Judgment and the resurrection in the natural body; but let those who have inward eyes look and discover therewith. They will understand that it has been called truly in the past a card of eternal life, and for this reason it may be compared with that which passes under the name of Temperance.

0 Zero The Fool

With light step, as if earth and its trammels had little power to restrain him, a young man in gorgeous vestments pauses at the brink of a precipice among the great heights of the world; he surveys the blue distance before him—its expanse of sky rather than the prospect below. His act of eager walking is still indicated, though he is stationary at the given moment; his dog is still bounding. The edge which opens on the depth has no terror; it is as if angels were waiting to uphold him, if it came about that he leaped from the height. His countenance is full of intelligence and expectant dream. He has a rose in one hand and in the other a costly wand, from which depends over his right shoulder a wallet curiously embroidered. He is a prince of the other world on his travels through this one—all amidst the morning glory, in the keen air. The sun, which shines behind him, knows whence he came, whither he is going, and how he will return by another path after many days. He is the spirit in search of experience.

XXI The World

The World represents the perfection and end of the Cosmos, the secret which is within it, the rapture of the universe when it understands itself in God. It is further the state of the soul in the consciousness of Divine Vision, reflected from the self-knowing spirit. It has more than one message on the macrocosmic side and is, for example, the state of the restored world when the law of manifestation shall have been carried to the highest degree of natural perfection. But it is perhaps more especially a story of the past, referring to that day when all was declared to be good, when the morning stars sang together and all the Sons of God shouted for joy. One of the worst explanations concerning it is that the figure symbolizes the Magus when he has reached the highest degree of initiation. The figure has been said to stand for Truth, which is, however, more properly allocated to the seventeenth card.

2. THE LESSER ARCANA

 The Suit of Wands

King

The physical and emotional nature to which this card is attributed is dark, ardent, lithe, animated, impassioned, noble. The King uplifts a flowering wand, and wears, like his three correspondences in the remaining suits, what is called a cap of maintenance beneath his crown. He connects with the symbol of the lion, which is emblazoned on the back of his throne. Divinatory Meanings: Dark man, friendly, countryman, generally married, honest and conscientious. The card always signifies honesty, and may mean news concerning an unexpected heritage to fall in before very long. Reversed: Good, but severe; austere, yet tolerant.

Queen

The Wands throughout this suit are always in leaf, as it is a suit of life and animation. Emotionally and otherwise, the Queen's personality corresponds to that of the King, but is more magnetic. Divinatory Meanings: A dark woman, countrywoman, friendly, chaste, loving, honourable. If the card beside her signifies a man, she is well disposed towards him; if a woman, she is interested in the Querent. Also, love of money, or a certain success in business. Reversed: Good, economical, obliging, serviceable. Signifies also—but in certain positions and in the neighbourhood of other cards tending in such directions—opposition, jealousy, even deceit and infidelity.

Knight

He is shewn as if upon a journey, armed with a short wand, and although mailed is not on a warlike errand. He is passing mounds or pyramids. The motion of the horse is a key to the character of its rider, and suggests the precipitate mood, or things connected therewith. Divinatory Meanings: Departure, absence, flight, emigration. A dark young man, friendly. Change of residence. Reversed: Rupture, division, interruption, discord.

Page
In a scene similar to the former, a young man stands in the act of proclamation. He is unknown but faithful, and his tidings are strange. Divinatory Meanings: Dark young man, faithful, a lover, an envoy, a postman. Beside a man, he will bear favourable testimony concerning him. A dangerous rival, if followed by the Page of Cups. Has the chief qualities of his suit. He may signify family intelligence. Reversed: Anecdotes, announcements, evil news. Also indecision and the instability which accompanies it.

Ten
A man oppressed by the weight of the ten staves which he is carrying. Divinatory Meanings: A card of many significances, and some of the readings cannot be harmonized. I set aside that which connects it with honour and good faith. The chief meaning is oppression simply, but it is also fortune, gain, any kind of success, and then it is the oppression of these things. It is also a card of false-seeming, disguise, perfidy. The place which the figure is approaching may suffer from the rods that he carries. Success is stultified if the Nine of Swords follows, and if it is a question of a lawsuit, there will be certain loss. Reversed: Contrarieties, difficulties, intrigues, and their analogies.

Nine
The figure leans upon his staff and has an expectant look, as if awaiting an enemy. Behind are eight other staves—erect, in orderly disposition, like a palisade. Divinatory Meanings: The card signifies strength in opposition. If attacked, the person will meet an onslaught boldly; and his build shews, that he may prove a formidable antagonist. With this main significance there are all its possible adjuncts—| delay, suspension, adjournment. Reversed: Obstacles, adversity, calamity.

Eight
The card represents motion through the immovable—a flight of wands through an open country; but they draw to the term of their course. That which they signify is at hand; it may be even on the threshold. Divinatory Meanings: Activity in undertakings, the path of such activity, swiftness, as that of an express messenger; great haste, great hope, speed towards an end which promises

assured felicity; generally, that which is on the move; also the arrows of love. Reversed: Arrows of jealousy, internal dispute, stingings of conscience, quarrels; and domestic disputes for persons who are married.

Seven
A young man on a craggy eminence brandishing a staff; six other staves are raised towards him from below. Divinatory Meanings: It is a card of valour, for, on the surface, six are attacking one, who has, however, the vantage position. On the intellectual plane, it signifies discussion, wordy strife; in business—negotiations, war of trade, barter, competition. It is further a card of success, for the combatant is on the top and his enemies may be unable to reach him. Reversed: Perplexity, embarrassments, anxiety. It is also a caution against indecision.

Six
A laurelled horseman bears one staff adorned with a laurel crown; footmen with staves are at his side. Divinatory Meanings: The card has been so designed that it can cover several significations; on the surface, it is a victor triumphing, but it is also great news, such as might be carried in state by the King's courier; it is expectation crowned with its own desire, the crown of hope, and so forth. Reversed: Apprehension, fear, as of a victorious enemy at the gate; treachery, disloyalty, as of gates being opened to the enemy; also indefinite delay.

Five
A posse of youths, who are brandishing staves, as if in sport or strife. It is mimic warfare, and hereto correspond the Divinatory Meanings: Imitation, as, for example, sham fight, but also the strenuous competition and struggle of the search after riches and fortune. In this sense it connects with the battle of life. Hence some attributions say that it is a card of gold, gain, opulence. Reversed: Litigation, disputes, trickery, contradiction.

Four
From the four great staves planted in the foreground there is a great garland suspended; two female figures uplift nosegays; at their side is a bridge over a moat, leading to an old manorial house. Divinatory Meanings: They are for once almost on the surface—country life, haven of refuge, a species of domestic harvest-home, repose, concord, harmony, prosperity, peace, and the perfected work

of these. Reversed: The meaning remains unaltered; it is prosperity, increase, felicity, beauty, embellishment.

Three
A calm, stately personage, with his back turned, looking from a cliff's edge at ships passing over the sea. Three staves are planted in the ground, and he leans slightly on one of them. Divinatory Meanings: He symbolizes established strength, enterprise, effort, trade, commerce, discovery; those are his ships, bearing his merchandise, which are sailing over the sea. The card also signifies able co-operation in business, as if the successful merchant prince were looking from his side towards yours with a view to help you. Reversed: The end of troubles, suspension or cessation of adversity, toil and disappointment.

Two
A tall man looks from a battlemented roof over sea and shore; he holds a globe in his right hand, while a staff in his left rests on the battlement; another is fixed in a ring. The Rose and Cross and Lily should be noticed on the left side. Divinatory Meanings: Between the alternative readings there is no marriage possible; on the one hand, riches, fortune, magnificence; on the other, physical suffering, disease, chagrin, sadness, mortification. The design gives one suggestion; here is a lord overlooking his dominion and alternately contemplating a globe; it looks like the malady, the mortification, the sadness of Alexander amidst the grandeur of this world's wealth. Reversed: Surprise, wonder, enchantment, emotion, trouble, fear.

Ace
A hand issuing from a cloud grasps a stout wand or club. Divinatory Meanings: Creation, invention, enterprise, the powers which result in these; principle, beginning, source; birth, family, origin, and in a sense the virility which is behind them; the starting point of enterprises; according to another account, money, fortune, inheritance. Reversed: Fall, decadence, ruin, perdition, to perish also a certain clouded joy.

The Suit of Cups

King

He holds a short sceptre in his left hand and a great cup in his right; his throne is set upon the sea; on one side a ship is riding and on the other a dolphin is leaping. The implicit is that the Sign of the Cup naturally refers to water, which appears in all the court cards. Divinatory Meanings: Fair man, man of business, law, or divinity; responsible, disposed to oblige the Querent; also equity, art and science, including those who profess science, law and art; creative intelligence. Reversed: Dishonest, double-dealing man; roguery, exaction, injustice, vice, scandal, pillage, considerable loss.

Queen

Beautiful, fair, dreamy—as one who sees visions in a cup. This is, however, only one of her aspects; she sees, but she also acts, and her activity feeds her dream. Divinatory Meanings: Good, fair woman; honest, devoted woman, who will do service to the Querent; loving intelligence, and hence the gift of vision; success, happiness, pleasure; also wisdom, virtue; a perfect spouse and a good mother. Reversed: The accounts vary; good woman; otherwise, distinguished woman but one not to be trusted; perverse woman; vice, dishonour, depravity.

Knight

Graceful, but not warlike; riding quietly, wearing a winged helmet, referring to those higher graces of the imagination which sometimes characterize this card. He too is a dreamer, but the images of the side of sense haunt him in his vision. Divinatory Meanings: Arrival, approach—sometimes that of a messenger; advances, proposition, demeanour, invitation, incitement. Reversed: Trickery, artifice, subtlety, swindling, duplicity, fraud.

Page

A fair, pleasing, somewhat effeminate page, of studious and intent aspect, contemplates a fish rising from a cup to look at him. It is the pictures of the mind taking form. Divinatory Meanings: Fair young man, one impelled to render service and with whom the Querent will be connected; a studious youth; news, message; application, reflection, meditation; also these things directed to business. Reversed: Taste, inclination, attachment, seduction, deception, artifice.

Ten

Appearance of Cups in a rainbow; it is contemplated in wonder and ecstacy by a man and woman below, evidently husband and wife. His right arm is about her; his left is raised upward; she raises her right arm. The two children dancing near them have not observed the prodigy but are happy after their own manner. There is a home-scene beyond. Divinatory Meanings: Contentment, repose of the entire heart; the perfection of that state; also perfection of human love and friendship; if with several picture-cards, a person who is taking charge of the Querent's interests; also the town, village or country inhabited by the Querent. Reversed: Repose of the false heart, indignation, violence.

Nine

A goodly personage has feasted to his heart's content, and abundant refreshment of wine is on the arched counter behind him, seeming to indicate that the future is also assured. The picture offers the material side only, but there are other aspects. Divinatory Meanings: Concord, contentment, physical bien-etre; also victory, success, advantage; satisfaction for the Querent or person for whom the consultation is made. Reversed: Truth, loyalty, liberty; but the readings vary and include mistakes, imperfections, etc.

Eight

A man of dejected aspect is deserting the cups of his felicity, enterprise, undertaking or previous concern. Divinatory Meanings: The card speaks for itself on the surface, but other readings are entirely antithetical—giving joy, mildness, timidity, honour, modesty. In practice, it is usually found that the card shews the decline of a matter, or that a matter which has been thought to be important is really of slight consequence—either for good or evil. Reversed: Great joy, happiness, feasting.

Seven
Strange chalices of vision, but the images are more especially those of the fantastic spirit. Divinatory Meanings: Fairy favours, images of reflection, sentiment, imagination, things seen in the glass of contemplation; some attainment in these degrees, but nothing permanent or substantial is suggested. Reversed: Desire, will, determination, project.

Six
Children in an old garden, their cups filled with flowers. Divinatory Meanings: A card of the past and of memories, looking back, as—for example—on childhood; happiness, enjoyment, but coming rather from the past; things that have vanished. Another reading reverses this, giving new relations, new knowledge, new environment, and then the children are disporting in an unfamiliar precinct. Reversed: The future, renewal, that which will come to pass presently.

Five
A dark, cloaked figure, looking sideways at three prone cups two others stand upright behind him; a bridge is in the background, leading to a small keep or holding. Divinatory Meanings: It is a card of loss, but something remains over; three have been taken, but two are left; it is a card of inheritance, patrimony, transmission, but not corresponding to expectations; with some interpreters it is a card of marriage, but not without bitterness or frustration. Reversed: News, alliances, affinity, consanguinity, ancestry, return, false projects.

Four
A young man is seated under a tree and contemplates three cups set on the grass before him; an arm issuing from a cloud offers him another cup. His expression notwithstanding is one of discontent with his environment. Divinatory Meanings: Weariness, disgust, aversion, imaginary vexations, as if the wine of this world had caused satiety only; another wine, as if a fairy gift, is now offered the wastrel, but he sees no consolation therein. This is also a card of blended pleasure. Reversed: Novelty, presage, new instruction, new relations.

Three

Maidens in a garden-ground with cups uplifted, as if pledging one another. Divinatory Meanings: The conclusion of any matter in plenty, perfection and merriment; happy issue, victory, fulfilment, solace, healing, Reversed: Expedition, dispatch, achievement, end. It signifies also the side of excess in physical enjoyment, and the pleasures of the senses.

Two

A youth and maiden are pledging one another, and above their cups rises the Caduceus of Hermes, between the great wings of which there appears a lion's head. It is a variant of a sign which is found in a few old examples of this card. Some curious emblematical meanings are attached to it, but they do not concern us in this place. Divinatory Meanings: Love, passion, friendship, affinity, union, concord, sympathy, the interrelation of the sexes, and—as a suggestion apart from all offices of divination—that desire which is not in Nature, but by which Nature is sanctified.

Ace

The waters are beneath, and thereon are water-lilies; the hand issues from the cloud, holding in its palm the cup, from which four streams are pouring; a dove, bearing in its bill a cross-marked Host, descends to place the Wafer in the Cup; the dew of water is falling on all sides. It is an intimation of that which may lie behind the Lesser Arcana. Divinatory Meanings: House of the true heart, joy, content, abode, nourishment, abundance, fertility; Holy Table, felicity hereof. Reversed: House of the false heart, mutation, instability, revolution.

The Suit of Swords

King
He sits in judgment, holding the unsheathed sign of his suit. He recalls, of course, the conventional Symbol of justice in the Trumps Major, and he may represent this virtue, but he is rather the power of life and death, in virtue of his office. Divinatory Meanings: Whatsoever arises out of the idea of judgment and all its connexions—power, command, authority, militant intelligence, law, offices of the crown, and so forth. Reversed: Cruelty, perversity, barbarity, perfidy, evil intention.

Queen
Her right hand raises the weapon vertically and the hilt rests on an arm of her royal chair the left hand is extended, the arm raised, her countenance is severe but chastened; it suggests familiarity with sorrow. It does not represent mercy and, her sword notwithstanding, she is scarcely a symbol of power. Divinatory Meanings: Widowhood, female sadness and embarrassment, absence, sterility, mourning, privation, separation. Reversed: Malice, bigotry, artifice, prudery, bale, deceit.

Knight
He is riding in full course, as if scattering his enemies. In the design he is really a prototypical hero of romantic chivalry. He might almost be Galahad, whose sword is swift and sure because he is clean of heart. Divinatory Meanings: Skill, bravery, capacity, defence, address, enmity, wrath, war, destruction, opposition, resistance, ruin. There is therefore a sense in which the card signifies death, but it carries this meaning only in its proximity to other cards of fatality. Reversed: Imprudence, incapacity, extravagance.

Page
A lithe, active figure holds a sword upright in both hands, while in the act of swift walking. He is passing over rugged land, and about his way the clouds

are collocated wildly. He is alert and lithe, looking this way and that, as if an expected enemy might appear at any moment. Divinatory Meanings: Authority, overseeing, secret service, vigilance, spying, examination, and the qualities thereto belonging. Reversed: More evil side of these qualities; what is unforeseen, unprepared state; sickness is also intimated.

Ten

A prostrate figure, pierced by all the swords belonging to the card. Divinatory Meanings: Whatsoever is intimated by the design; also pain, affliction, tears, sadness, desolation. It is not especially a card of violent death. Reversed: Advantage, profit, success, favour, but none of these are permanent; also power and authority.

Nine

One seated on her couch in lamentation, with the swords over her. She is as one who knows no sorrow which is like unto hers. It is a card of utter desolation. Divinatory Meanings: Death, failure, miscarriage, delay, deception, disappointment, despair. Reversed: Imprisonment, suspicion, doubt, reasonable fear, shame.

Eight

A woman, bound and hoodwinked, with the swords of the card about her. Yet it is rather a card of temporary durance than of irretrievable bondage. Divinatory Meanings: Bad news, violent chagrin, crisis, censure, power in trammels, conflict, calumny; also sickness. Reversed: Disquiet, difficulty, opposition, accident, treachery; what is unforeseen; fatality.

Seven

A man in the act of carrying away five swords rapidly; the two others of the card remain stuck in the ground. A camp is close at hand. Divinatory Meanings: Design, attempt, wish, hope, confidence; also quarrelling, a plan that may fail, annoyance. The design is uncertain in its import, because the significations are widely at variance with each other. Reversed: Good advice, counsel, instruction, slander, babbling.

Six

A ferryman carrying passengers in his punt to the further shore. The course is smooth, and seeing that the freight is light, it may be noted that the work is not beyond his strength. Divinatory Meanings: journey by water, route, way, envoy, commissionary, expedient. Reversed: Declaration, confession, publicity; one account says that it is a proposal of love.

Five
A disdainful man looks after two retreating and dejected figures. Their swords lie upon the ground. He carries two others on his left shoulder, and a third sword is in his right hand, point to earth. He is the master in possession of the field. Divinatory Meanings: Degradation, destruction, revocation, infamy, dishonour, loss, with the variants and analogues of these. Reversed: The same; burial and obsequies.

Four
The effigy of a knight in the attitude of prayer, at full length upon his tomb. Divinatory Meanings: Vigilance, retreat, solitude, hermit's repose, exile, tomb and coffin. It is these last that have suggested the design. Reversed: Wise administration, circumspection, economy, avarice, precaution, testament.

Three
Three swords piercing a heart; cloud and rain behind. Divinatory Meanings: Removal, absence, delay, division, rupture, dispersion, and all that the design signifies naturally, being too simple and obvious to call for specific enumeration. Reversed: Mental alienation, error, loss, distraction, disorder, confusion.

Two
A hoodwinked female figure balances two swords upon her shoulders. Divinatory Meanings: Conformity and the equipoise which it suggests, courage, friendship, concord in a state of arms; another reading gives tenderness, affection, intimacy. The suggestion of harmony and other favourable readings must be considered in a qualified manner, as Swords generally are not symbolical of beneficent forces in human affairs. Reversed: Imposture, falsehood, duplicity, disloyalty.

Ace
A hand issues from a cloud, grasping as word, the point of which is encircled by a crown. Divinatory Meanings: Triumph, the excessive degree in everything, conquest, triumph of force. It is a card of great force, in love as well as in hatred. The crown may carry a much higher significance than comes usually within the sphere of fortune-telling. Reversed: The same, but the results are disastrous; another account says—conception, childbirth, augmentation, multiplicity.

The Suit of Pentacles

King

The bull's head should be noted as a recurrent symbol on the throne. The sign of this suit is represented throughout as engraved or blazoned with the pentagram, typifying the correspondence of the four elements in human nature and that by which they may be governed. In many old Tarot packs this suit stood for current coin, money, deniers. I have not invented the substitution of pentacles and I have no special cause to sustain in respect of the alternative. But the consensus of divinatory meanings is on the side of some change, because the cards do not happen to deal especially with questions of money. Divinatory Meanings: Valour, realizing intelligence, business and normal intellectual aptitude, sometimes mathematical gifts and attainments of this kind; success in these paths. Reversed: Vice, weakness, ugliness, perversity, corruption, peril.

Queen

The face suggests that of a dark woman, whose qualities might be summed up in the idea of greatness of soul; she has also the serious cast of intelligence; she contemplates her symbol and may see worlds therein. Divinatory Meanings: Opulence, generosity, magnificence, security, liberty. Reversed: Evil, suspicion, suspense, fear, mistrust.

Knight

He rides a slow, enduring, heavy horse, to which his own aspect corresponds. He exhibits his symbol, but does not look therein. Divinatory Meanings: Utility, serviceableness, interest, responsibility, rectitude-all on the normal and external plane. Reversed: inertia, idleness, repose of that kind, stagnation; also placidity, discouragement, carelessness.

Page

A youthful figure, looking intently at the pentacle which hovers over his raised hands. He moves slowly, insensible of that which is about him. Divinatory

Meanings: Application, study, scholarship, reflection another reading says news, messages and the bringer thereof; also rule, management. Reversed: Prodigality, dissipation, liberality, luxury; unfavourable news.

Ten

A man and woman beneath an archway which gives entrance to a house and domain. They are accompanied by a child, who looks curiously at two dogs accosting an ancient personage seated in the foreground. The child's hand is on one of them. Divinatory Meanings: Gain, riches; family matters, archives, extraction, the abode of a family. Reversed: Chance, fatality, loss, robbery, games of hazard; sometimes gift, dowry, pension.

Nine

A woman, with a bird upon her wrist, stands amidst a great abundance of grape-vines in the garden of a manorial house. It is a wide domain, suggesting plenty in all things. Possibly it is her own possession and testifies to material well-being. Divinatory Meanings: Prudence, safety, success, accomplishment, certitude, discernment. Reversed: Roguery, deception, voided project, bad faith.

Eight

An artist in stone at his work, which he exhibits in the form of trophies. Divinatory Meanings: Work, employment, commission, craftsmanship, skill in craft and business, perhaps in the preparatory stage. Reversed: Voided ambition, vanity, cupidity, exaction, usury. It may also signify the possession of skill, in the sense of the ingenious mind turned to cunning and intrigue.

Seven

A young man, leaning on his staff, looks intently at seven pentacles attached to a clump of greenery on his right; one would say that these were his treasures and that his heart was there. Divinatory Meanings: These are exceedingly contradictory; in the main, it is a card of money, business, barter; but one reading gives altercation, quarrels—and another innocence, ingenuity, purgation. Reversed: Cause for anxiety regarding money which it may be proposed to lend.

Six

A person in the guise of a merchant weighs money in a pair of scales and distributes it to the needy and distressed. It is a testimony to his own success in life, as well as to his goodness of heart. Divinatory Meanings: Presents, gifts, gratification another account says attention, vigilance now is the accepted time, present prosperity, etc. Reversed: Desire, cupidity, envy, jealousy, illusion.

FIVE
Two mendicants in a snow-storm pass a lighted casement. Divinatory Meanings: The card foretells material trouble above all, whether in the form illustrated—that is, destitution—or otherwise. For some cartomancists, it is a card of love and lovers-wife, husband, friend, mistress; also concordance, affinities. These alternatives cannot be harmonized. Reversed: Disorder, chaos, ruin, discord, profligacy.

FOUR
A crowned figure, having a pentacle over his crown, clasps another with hands and arms; two pentacles are under his feet. He holds to that which he has. Divinatory Meanings: The surety of possessions, cleaving to that which one has, gift, legacy, inheritance. Reversed: Suspense, delay, opposition.

THREE
A sculptor at his work in a monastery. Compare the design which illustrates the Eight of Pentacles. The apprentice or amateur therein has received his reward and is now at work in earnest. Divinatory Meanings: Metier, trade, skilled labour; usually, however, regarded as a card of nobility, aristocracy, renown, glory. Reversed: Mediocrity, in work and otherwise, puerility, pettiness, weakness.

TWO
A young man, in the act of dancing, has a pentacle in either hand, and they are joined by that endless cord which is like the number 8 reversed. Divinatory Meanings: On the one hand it is represented as a card of gaiety, recreation and its connexions, which is the subject of the design; but it is read also as news and messages in writing, as obstacles, agitation, trouble, embroilment. Reversed: Enforced gaiety, simulated enjoyment, literal sense, handwriting, composition, letters of exchange.

ACE
A hand—issuing, as usual, from a cloud—holds up a pentacle. Divinatory Meanings: Perfect contentment, felicity, ecstasy; also speedy intelligence; gold. Reversed: The evil side of wealth, bad intelligence; also great riches. In any case it shews prosperity, comfortable material conditions, but whether these are of advantage to the possessor will depend on whether the card is reversed or not.

3. THE GREATER ARCANA AND THEIR DIVINATORY MEANINGS

Such are the intimations of the Lesser Arcana in respect of divinatory art, the veridic nature of which seems to depend on an alternative that it may be serviceable to express briefly. The records of the art are ex hypothesi the records of findings in the past based upon experience; as such, they are a guide to memory, and those who can master the elements may—still ex hypothesi—give interpretations on their basis. It is an official and automatic working. On the other hand, those who have gifts of intuition, of second sight, of clairvoyance—call it as we choose and may—will supplement the experience of the past by the findings of their own faculty, and will speak of that which they have seen in the pretexts of the oracles. It remains to give, also briefly, the divinatory significance allocated by the same art to the Trumps Major.

1. THE MAGICIAN—Skill, diplomacy, address, subtlety; sickness, pain, loss, disaster, snares of enemies; self-confidence, will; the Querent, if male. Reversed: Physician, Magus, mental disease, disgrace, disquiet.

2. THE HIGH PRIESTESS—Secrets, mystery, the future as yet unrevealed; the woman who interests the Querent, if male; the Querent herself, if female; silence, tenacity; mystery, wisdom, science. Reversed: Passion, moral or physical ardour, conceit, surface knowledge.

3. THE EMPRESS—Fruitfulness, action, initiative, length of days; the unknown, clandestine; also difficulty, doubt, ignorance. Reversed: Light, truth, the unravelling of involved matters, public rejoicings; according to another reading, vacillation.

4. THE EMPEROR—Stability, power, protection, realization; a great person; aid, reason, conviction; also authority and will. Reversed: Benevolence, compassion, credit; also confusion to enemies, obstruction, immaturity.

5. THE HIEROPHANT—Marriage, alliance, captivity, servitude; by another account, mercy and goodness; inspiration; the man to whom the Querent has recourse. Reversed: Society, good understanding, concord, overkindness, weakness.

6. THE LOVERS—Attraction, love, beauty, trials overcome. Reversed: Failure, foolish designs. Another account speaks of marriage frustrated and contrarieties of all kinds.

7. THE CHARIOT—Succour, providence also war, triumph, presumption, vengeance, trouble. Reversed: Riot, quarrel, dispute, litigation, defeat.

8. STRENGTH—Power, energy, action, courage, magnanimity; also complete success and honours. Reversed: Despotism, abuse if power, weakness, discord, sometimes even disgrace.

9. THE HERMIT—Prudence, circumspection; also and especially treason, dissimulation, roguery, corruption. Reversed: Concealment, disguise, policy, fear, unreasoned caution.

10. WHEEL OF FORTUNE—Destiny, fortune, success, elevation, luck, felicity. Reversed: Increase, abundance, superfluity.

11. JUSTICE—Equity, rightness, probity, executive; triumph of the deserving side in law. Reversed: Law in all its departments, legal complications, bigotry, bias, excessive severity.

12. THE HANGED MAN—Wisdom, circumspection, discernment, trials, sacrifice, intuition, divination, prophecy. Reversed: Selfishness, the crowd, body politic.

13. DEATH—End, mortality, destruction, corruption also, for a man, the loss of a benefactor for a woman, many contrarieties; for a maid, failure of marriage projects. Reversed: Inertia, sleep, lethargy, petrifaction, somnambulism; hope destroyed.

14. TEMPERANCE—Economy, moderation, frugality, management, accommodation. Reversed: Things connected with churches, religions, sects, the priesthood, sometimes even the priest who will marry the Querent; also disunion, unfortunate combinations, competing interests.

15. THE DEVIL—Ravage, violence, vehemence, extraordinary efforts, force, fatality; that which is predestined but is not for this reason evil. Reversed: Evil fatality, weakness, pettiness, blindness.

16. THE TOWER—Misery, distress, indigence, adversity, calamity, disgrace, deception, ruin. It is a card in particular of unforeseen catastrophe. Reversed: According to one account, the same in a lesser degree also oppression, imprisonment, tyranny.

17. THE STAR—Loss, theft, privation, abandonment; another reading says hope and bright prospects, Reversed: Arrogance, haughtiness, impotence.

18. THE MOON—Hidden enemies, danger, calumny, darkness, terror, deception, occult forces, error. Reversed: Instability, inconstancy, silence, lesser degrees of deception and error.

19. THE SUN—Material happiness, fortunate marriage, contentment. Reversed: The same in a lesser sense.

20. JUDGEMENT—Change of position, renewal, outcome. Another account specifies total loss though lawsuit. Reversed: Weakness, pusillanimity, simplicity; also deliberation, decision, sentence.

21. (ZERO) THE FOOL—Folly, mania, extravagance, intoxication, delirium, frenzy, bewrayment. Reversed: Negligence, absence, distribution, carelessness, apathy, nullity, vanity.

22. (21.) THE WORLD—Assured success, recompense, voyage, route, emigration, flight, change of place. Reversed: Inertia, fixity, stagnation, permanence.

4. SOME ADDITIONAL MEANINGS OF THE LESSER ARCANA

Wands

King: Generally favourable may signify a good marriage. Reversed: Advice that should be followed.

Queen: A good harvest, which may be taken in several senses. Reversed: Goodwill towards the Querent, but without the opportunity to exercise it.

Knight: A bad card; according to some readings, alienation. Reversed: For a woman, marriage, but probably frustrated.

Page: Young man of family in search of young lady. Reversed: Bad news.

Ten: Difficulties and contradictions, if near a good card.

Nine: Generally speaking, a bad card.

Eight: Domestic disputes for a married person.

Seven: A dark child.

Six: Servants may lose the confidence of their masters; a young lady may be betrayed by a friend. Reversed: Fulfilment of deferred hope.

Five: Success in financial speculation. Reversed: Quarrels may be turned to advantage.

Four: Unexpected good fortune. Reversed: A married woman will have beautiful children.

Three: A very good card; collaboration will favour enterprise.

Two: A young lady may expect trivial disappointments.

Ace: Calamities of all kinds. Reversed: A sign of birth.

CUPS

King: Beware of ill-will on the part of a man of position, and of hypocrisy pretending to help. Reversed: Loss.

Queen: Sometimes denotes a woman of equivocal character. Reversed: A rich marriage for a man and a distinguished one for a woman.

Knight: A visit from a friend, who will bring unexpected money to the Querent. Reversed: Irregularity.

Page: Good augury; also a young man who is unfortunate in love. Reversed: Obstacles of all kinds.

Ten: For a male Querent, a good marriage and one beyond his expectations. Reversed: Sorrow; also a serious quarrel.

Nine: Of good augury for military men. Reversed: Good business.

Eight: Marriage with a fair woman. Reversed: Perfect satisfaction.

Seven: Fair child; idea, design, resolve, movement. Reversed: Success, if accompanied by the Three of Cups.

Six: Pleasant memories. Reversed: Inheritance to fall in quickly.

Five: Generally favourable; a happy marriage; also patrimony, legacies, gifts, success in enterprise. Reversed: Return of some relative who has not been seen for long.

Four: Contrarieties. Reversed: Presentiment.

Three: Unexpected advancement for a military man. Reversed: Consolation, cure, end of the business.

Two: Favourable in things of pleasure and business, as well as love; also wealth and honour. Reversed: Passion.

Ace: Inflexible will, unalterable law. Reversed: Unexpected change of position.

Swords

King: A lawyer, senator, doctor. Reversed: A bad man; also a caution to put an end to a ruinous lawsuit.

Queen: A widow. Reversed: A bad woman, with ill-will towards the Querent.

Knight: A soldier, man of arms, satellite, stipendiary; heroic action predicted for soldier. Reversed: Dispute with an imbecile person; for a woman, struggle with a rival, who will be conquered.

Page: An indiscreet person will pry into the Querent's secrets. Reversed: Astonishing news.

Ten: Followed by Ace and King, imprisonment; for girl or wife, treason on the part of friends. Reversed: Victory and consequent fortune for a soldier in war.

Nine: An ecclesiastic, a priest; generally, a card of bad omen. Reversed: Good ground for suspicion against a doubtful person.

Eight: For a woman, scandal spread in her respect. Reversed: Departure of a relative.

Seven: Dark girl; a good card; it promises a country life after a competence has been secured. Reversed: Good advice, probably neglected.

Six: The voyage will be pleasant. Reversed: Unfavourable issue of lawsuit.

Five: An attack on the fortune of the Querent. Reversed: A sign of sorrow and mourning.

Four: A bad card, but if reversed a qualified success may be expected by wise administration of affairs. Reversed: A certain success following wise administration.

Three: For a woman, the flight of her lover. Reversed: A meeting with one whom the Querent has compromised; also a nun.

Two: Gifts for a lady, influential protection for a man in search of help. Reversed: Dealings with rogues.

Ace: Great prosperity or great misery. Reversed: Marriage broken off, for a woman, through her own imprudence.

Pentacles

King: A rather dark man, a merchant, master, professor. Reversed: An old and vicious man.

Queen: Dark woman; presents from a rich relative; rich and happy marriage for a young man. Reversed: An illness.

Knight: An useful man; useful discoveries. Reversed: A brave man out of employment.

Page: A dark youth; a young officer or soldier; a child. Reversed: Sometimes degradation and sometimes pillage.

Ten: Represents house or dwelling, and derives its value from other cards. Reversed: An occasion which may be fortunate or otherwise.

Nine: Prompt fulfilment of what is presaged by neighbouring cards. Reversed: Vain hopes.

Eight: A young man in business who has relations with the Querent; a dark girl. Reversed: The Querent will be compromised in a matter of money-lending.

Seven: Improved position for a lady's future husband. Reversed: Impatience, apprehension, suspicion.

Six: The present must not be relied on. Reversed: A check on the Querent's ambition.

Five: Conquest of fortune by reason. Reversed: Troubles in love.

Four: For a bachelor, pleasant news from a lady. Reversed: Observation, hindrances.

Three: If for a man, celebrity for his eldest son. Reversed: Depends on neighbouring cards.

Two: Troubles are more imaginary than real. Reversed: Bad omen, ignorance, injustice.

Ace: The most favourable of all cards. Reversed: A share in the finding of treasure.

5. THE RECURRENCE OF CARDS IN DEALING

In the Natural Position:

4 Kings = great honour; 3 Kings = consultation; 2 Kings = minor counsel.

4 Queens = great debate; 3 Queens = deception by women; 2 Queens = sincere friends.

4 Knights = serious matters; 3 Knights = lively debate; 2 Knights = intimacy.

4 Pages = dangerous illness; 3 Pages = dispute; 2 Pages = disquiet.

4 Tens = condemnation; 3 Tens = new condition; 2 Tens = change.

4 Nines = a good friend; 3 Nines = success; 2 Nines = receipt.

4 Eights = reverse; 3 Eights = marriage 2 Eights = new knowledge.

4 Sevens = intrigue; 3 Sevens = infirmity; 2 Sevens = news.

4 Sixes = abundance; 3 Sixes = success; 2 Sixes = irritability.

4 Fives = regularity; 3 Fives = determination; 2 Fives = vigils.

4 Fours = journey near at hand; 3 Fours = a subject of reflection; 2 Fours = insomnia.

4 Threes = progress; 3 Threes = unity 2 Threes = calm.

4 Twos = contention; 3 Twos = security; 2 Twos = accord.

4 Aces = favourable chance; 3 Aces = small success; 2 Aces = trickery.

Reversed:

4 Kings = celerity; 3 Kings = commerce 2 Kings = projects.

4 Queens = bad company; 3 Queens = gluttony; 2 Queens = work.

4 Knights = alliance 3 Knights = a duel, or personal encounter; 2 Knights = susceptibility.

4 Pages = privation 3 Pages = idleness 2 Pages = society.

4 Tens = event, happening; 3 Tens disappointment; 2 Tens = expectation justified.

4 Nines = usury; 3 Nines imprudence; 2 Nines = a small profit.

4 Eights = error; 3 Eights a spectacle; 2 Eights = misfortune.

4 Sevens = quarrellers; 3 Sevens = joy; 2 Sevens = women of no repute.

4 Sixes = care; 3 Sixes = satisfaction 2 Sixes = downfall.

4 Fives = order; 3 Fives = hesitation; 2 Fives = reverse.

4 Fours = walks abroad; 3 Fours = disquiet; 2 Fours = dispute.

4 Threes = great success; 3 Threes = serenity; 2 Threes = safety.

4 Twos = reconciliation; 3 Twos apprehension; 2 Twos = mistrust.

4 Aces = dishonour; 3 Aces debauchery; 2 Aces = enemies.

6. THE ART OF TAROT DIVINATION

We come now to the final and practical part of this division of our subject, being the way to consult and obtain oracles by means of Tarot cards. The modes of operation are rather numerous, and some of them are exceedingly involved. I set aside those last mentioned, because persons who are versed in such questions believe that the way of simplicity is the way of truth. I set aside also the operations which have been republished recently in that section of *The Tarot of the Bohemians* which is entitled "The Divining Tarot"; it may be recommended at its proper value to readers who wish to go further than the limits of this handbook. I offer in the first place a short process which has been used privately for many years past in England, Scotland and Ireland. I believe that it will serve all purposes.

7. AN ANCIENT CELTIC METHOD OF DIVINATION

This mode of divination is the most suitable for obtaining an answer to a definite question. The Diviner first selects a card to represent the person or, matter about which inquiry is made. This card is called the Significator. Should he wish to ascertain something in connexion with himself he takes the one which corresponds to his personal description. A Knight should be chosen as the Significator if the subject of inquiry is a man of forty years old and upward; a King should be chosen for any male who is under that age; a Queen for a woman who is over forty years and a Page for any female of less age.

The four Court Cards in Wands represent very fair people, with yellow or auburn hair, fair complexion and blue eyes. The Court Cards in Cups signify people with light brown or dull fair hair and grey or blue eyes. Those in Swords stand for people having hazel or grey eyes, dark brown hair and dull complexion. Lastly, the Court Cards in Pentacles are referred to persons with very dark brown or black hair, dark eyes and sallow or swarthy complexions. These allocations are subject, however, to the following reserve, which will prevent them being taken too conventionally. You can be guided on occasion by the known temperament of a person; one who is exceedingly dark may be very energetic, and would be better represented by a Sword card than a Pentacle. On the other hand, a very fair subject who is indolent and lethargic should be referred to Cups rather than to Wands.

If it is more convenient for the purpose of a divination to take as the Significator the matter about which inquiry is to be made, that Trump or small card should be selected which has a meaning corresponding to the matter. Let it be supposed that the question is: Will a lawsuit be necessary? In this case, take the Trump No. 11, or Justice, as the Significator. This has reference to legal affairs. But if the question is: Shall I be successful in my lawsuit? one of the Court Cards must be chosen as the Significator. Subsequently, consecutive divinations may be performed to ascertain the course of the process itself and its result to each of the parties concerned.

Having selected the Significator, place it on the table, face upwards. Then shuffle and cut the rest of the pack three times, keeping the faces of the cards downwards.

Turn up the top or FIRST CARD of the pack; cover the Significator with it, and say: This covers him. This card gives the influence which is affecting the person or matter of inquiry generally, the atmosphere of it in which the other currents work.

Turn up the SECOND CARD and lay it across the FIRST, saying: This crosses him. It shews the nature of the obstacles in the matter. If it is a favourable card, the opposing forces will not be serious, or it may indicate that something good in itself will not be productive of good in the particular connexion.

Turn up the THIRD CARD; place it above the Significator, and say: This crowns him. It represents (a) the Querent's aim or ideal in the matter; (b) the best that can be achieved under the circumstances, but that which has not yet been made actual.

Turn up the FOURTH CARD; place it below the Significator, and say: This is beneath him. It shews the foundation or basis of the matter, that which has already passed into actuality and which the Significator has made his own.

Turn up the FIFTH CARD; place it on the side of the Significator from which he is looking, and say: This is behind him. It gives the influence that is just passed, or is now passing away.

N.B.—If the Significator is a Trump or any small card that cannot be said to face either way, the Diviner must decide before beginning the operation which side he will take it as facing.

Turn up the SIXTH CARD; place it on the side that the Significator is facing, and say: This is before him. It shews the influence that is coming into action and will operate in the near future.

The cards are now disposed in the form of a cross, the Significator—covered by the First Card—being in the centre.

The next four cards are turned up in succession and placed one above the other in a line, on the right hand side of the cross.

The first of these, or the SEVENTH CARD of the operation, signifies himself—that is, the Significator—whether person or thing-and shews its position or attitude in the circumstances.

The EIGHTH CARD signifies his house, that is, his environment and the tendencies at work therein which have an effect on the matter—for instance, his position in life, the influence of immediate friends, and so forth.

The NINTH CARD gives his hopes or fears in the matter.

The TENTH is what will come, the final result, the culmination which is brought about by the influences shewn by the other cards that have been turned up in the divination.

It is on this card that the Diviner should especially concentrate his intuitive faculties and his memory in respect of the official divinatory meanings attached thereto. It should embody whatsoever you may have divined from the other cards on the table, including the Significator itself and concerning him or it, not excepting such lights upon higher significance as might fall like sparks from heaven if the card which serves for the oracle, the card for reading, should happen to be a Trump Major.

The operation is now completed; but should it happen that the last card is of a dubious nature, from which no final decision can be drawn, or which does not appear to indicate the ultimate conclusion of the affair, it may be well to repeat the operation, taking in this case the Tenth Card as the Significator, instead of the one previously used. The pack must be again shuffled and cut three times and the first ten cards laid out as before. By this a more detailed account of "What will come" may be obtained.

If in any divination the Tenth Card should be a Court Card, it shews that the subject of the divination falls ultimately into the hands of a person represented by that card, and its end depends mainly on him. In this event also it is useful to take the Court Card in question as the Significator in a fresh operation, and discover what is the nature of his influence in the matter and to what issue he will bring it.

Great facility may be obtained by this method in a comparatively short time, allowance being always made for the gifts of the operator—that is to say, his faculty of insight, latent or developed—and it has the special advantage of being free from all complications.

I here append a diagram of the cards as laid out in this mode of divination. The Significator is here covered by card 1.

The Significator.

1. That covers him.

2. What crosses him.

3. What crowns him.

4. What is beneath him.

5. What is behind him.

6. What is before him.

7. Himself.

8. His house.

9. His hopes or fears.

10. What will come.